Motivation Behind the Creation and Relevance of the IMF in a Globalized World

Dedicated to

Henry Chibuikem Irobiko

Table of Contents

FOREWORD BY THE AUTHOR

While acknowledging the plausible work done by the IMF and its counterpart the World Bank in facilitating global financial markets regulation and prevention of financial sector abuse, as oversight institutions, they need to constantly review their mandate to respond robustly to their dynamic challenges such as the global and debt crises and financial sector abuse. Oversight institutions need to constantly review and adapt their mandate accordingly if they are to discharge their varied responsibilities efficiently. They cannot stand still in the face of challenges because they will be superseded and kept at a back foot.

Markets and states are embedded in each other, and the way they are regulated is of a significant importance to varied stakeholders and people.

This paper is one of its kind, is unique in its character and evaluates embedded issues using empirical evidence in a way not done in its context before. Secondary data sources have been evaluated to achieve a thoughtful analysis of the objectives of the paper.

Executive Summary

Discussions on globalization always orbit the International Monetary Fund (IMF). In the last two decades, the IMF has taken blames for recurring financial crises around the world (Mansor et al., 2019). But globalization is as old as history whereas the IMF has evolved over time although the organization's contributions to the development of global economies have been a source of controversy. In this study, the IMF is viewed as an international financier aiming to control the excesses of globalization. Crisis management and sustenance of economic growth among nations are the major tasks but how the IMF has achieved these goals is subject to analysis (Howell., 1995).

Keywords: IMF, World Bank, EU, United States, global finance, financial crisis, economic growth, globalization, crisis management, international trade, leadership, and strategic management.

Chapter 1

1.0 Introduction

Globalization is a multifaceted concept often used in business and international relations to connote foreign trade, liberalization, and global finance. It refers to the free movement of people, goods, and services in a more integrated, hassle-free manner. According to Amal and Kang (2019), this interconnectedness benefits global economies in different ways, with more unfavourable consequences for developing nations, particularly because—in line with the theory of competitive advantage—trade relations between countries tend to favour financially-buoyant producing and exporting nations who easily exploit sales opportunities in international markets. Issues of neo-colonialism and political dominance are also synonymous with globalization (Ahmed & Brennan., 2019; Ahmed & Brennan, 2019; Bond, 2019).

However, countries involved in global trade are—in theory—subject to some rules and regulations implemented by the World Trade Organization (WTO) which monitors adherence to the trade agreements (terms and conditions) between and among countries. Although world organizations like the United Nations (UN) act as an arbitration body that oversees policies guiding free and non-discriminatory trade, the International Monetary Fund (IMF) aims at boosting national economies, reducing price of consumer goods and eliminating poverty around the world (Samiee., 2019; Brown & Bulman, 2006; Calle et al, 2019. Elleuch & Taktak, 2015).

The IMF has, so far, rendered financial support to ailing economies as well as ensured that financial activities of capitalist nations are controlled (Zoega., 2018). This study critically examines the rationale behind creation of the IMF, including how the international organization has fared in its roles.

1.0.1 FUNCTIONAL DEPARTMENTS

The IMF has three principal functions and activities: surveillance of financial and monetary conditions in its member countries and of the world economy. providing financial assistance to help countries overcome major balance of payment problems, and technical assistance and advisory services to member countries.

Functional Departments of the IMF

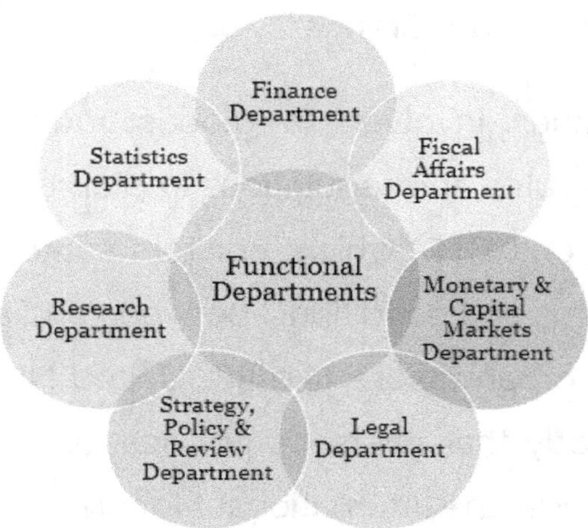

Source: IMF (2019)

General functions of the IMF are as follows:

- ✓ It works to foster global growth and economic stability.

- ✓ It helps to achieve macroeconomic stability and reduce poverty.

- ✓ The IMF provides alternative sources of financing.

- ✓ It oversees the fixed exchange rate agreements between countries.

- ✓ It helps national governments to manage their exchange rates and allows these governments to prioritize economic growth.

- ✓ It helps to provide short-term capital to aid the balance of payments.

- ✓ The IMF was also intended to help mend the pieces of the global economy after the Great Depression and World War II.

- ✓ To provide capital investments for economic growth and projects such as infrastructure.

- ✓ To examine the economic policies of countries with IMF loan agreements to determine if a shortage of capital was due to economic fluctuations or economic policy.

- ✓ The IMF also researches what types of government policy would ensure economic recovery.

- ✓ A particular concern of the IMF was to prevent financial crisis, from spreading and threatening the entire global financial/currency system.

- ✓ The IMF negotiates conditions on lending and loans under their policy of conditionality.

1.0.2 PURPOSE OF THE IMF

- Promote international monetary cooperation.

- Expansion and balanced growth of international trade.

- Promote exchange rate stability.

- Eliminate restrictions on the international flow of capital.

- Make resources of the fund available to the members.

- Help to establish multilateral system of payments and eliminate foreign exchange restrictions.

- Shorten the duration and lessen the degree of disequilibrium in international balances of payment.

- Foster economic growth and high levels of payment.

- Provide temporary financial assistance to countries to adjust balance of payments.

1.0.3 SUCCESSES OF THE IMF

a) International monetary corporation.

b) Multilateral system of foreign payments.

c) Reconstruction of European countries.

d) Increase in international Liquidity.

e) Increase in international trade.

f) Special aid to developing countries.

g) Providing statistical information.

h) Helpful in times of economic/financial difficulties.

i) Easiness and flexibility in making international payments.

1.0.4 FAILURES OF THE IMF

a) Lack of stability in the price of gold.

b) Lack of stability in exchange rate.

c) Inability to remove restrictions on foreign trade.

d) Rich nations club.

e) No help for development projects.

f) No solution of international liquidity.

g) Interference in domestic economies.

h) Inability to tackle the Monetary Crisis of August 1971.

i) Less aid for developing countries.

j)   High rate of interest.

1.0.5 Facts About the IMF

The primary purpose of the IMF is to safeguard the stability of international monetary system - that is, the system of exchange rates and international payments that enables countries (and their citizens) to buy goods and services from each other.

The IMF works to foster global growth and economic stability. It provides policy advice and financing to member countries in economic distress and collaborate closely with developing nations to help them achieve macroeconomic stability as well as reduce poverty.

Notable facts about the IMF include:

a) IMF is an abbreviation for the International Monetary Fund.

b) Formation: It was established on 7 July 1944.

c) Type of organization: International financial institution.

d) Purpose: Promote international monetary cooperation, facilitate international trade, foster sustainable economic growth, and make resources available to members experiencing balance of payment difficulties.

e) Membership: 189 countries.

f)   Headquarters: Washington D.C., United States.

g) Main organ: Board of governors.

h) Parent organization: United Nations.

i) Managing Director: Kristalina Georgieva

j) Staff: 3,000 employees from more than 160 countries who represent a world of cultures, backgrounds, and skills that strive to live core Fund values of excellence, honesty, impartiality, inclusion, integrity, and respect.

k) Argentina's debt to the IMF is equivalent to 5.3% of the country's GDP. In total, the country owns more than $32 billion.

l) Kristalina Georgieva is a former Vice-President of the European Commission for Budget & Human Resources (HR). She was previously CEO of the World Bank (2017-2019) during which time she served as Interim President of the World Bank Group for three months. She helped shape the agenda of the European Union in her role as European Commission Vice President for Budget and Human Resources (2014-2016) and as Commissioner for International Cooperation, Humanitarian Aid and Crisis Response (2010-2014). She began her career in public service at the World Bank as an Environmental Economist in 1993 where she went on to serve for 17 years in senior positions including Vice President and Corporate Secretary (2008-2010). Kristalina holds a PhD in Economic Science from the University of National and World Economy in Bulgaria.

1.1 Aim of the Study

The aim of this research is to contribute to knowledge by exploring the past and current impact of IMF on global economies. Achieving this aim is predicated on stating of relevant objectives as appear below:

1.2 Objectives of the Research

To achieve the research aim stated above, the relevant research objectives are.

1. To undertake a critical review of literature on IMF, with focus on how it has contributed to the development of nations.

2. To identify and critically analyse key constraints and success factors of the global financial institution.

3. To analyse historical trends in IMF's economic partnerships with developing countries.

1.3 Research Method

The alignment of research philosophy with the stated aim and objectives of research is important in any study and determines the outcome of study. This study will adopt the pragmatism research philosophy. Bhattacharjee (2012) expressed that the pragmatism philosophic strain combines elements of positivist and interpretive methods. The adopted philosophy will allow the researcher to make different linkages between theory and data and utilize such linkages in achieving the objectives of this study.

Chapter 2

2.0 ANALYSIS AND DISCUSSION

2.1 AN OVERVIEW OF GLOBALIZATION

Globalization is an outcome of the search for new markets in the post-World War II era, starting from the 44-nation Bretton Woods agreement of 1944 which established mercantilist trade and international commodity markets. Glynn (2007) notes that theories of capitalism and socialism have acknowledged the need for nations to accumulate and distribute wealth through multinational corporations, exports, and foreign direct investments (FDIs) since the industrial revolution. This interconnectivity is evident in technology-empowered advancements in science, transportation, communication, banking, and ICT, among others. Globalization is therefore a result of specially formulated plans and targeted neo-liberal laws, including other economic, socio-cultural, and political measures designed to promote market capitalism. Ronald Reagan's administration in the US and Margaret Thatcher's regime in the UK, thus, championed the course of globalization by setting up debt cancelation processes and structural advancement programs for developing economies—to create financial stability (Bond., 2019). This led to the birth of the IMF and World Bank (Calle et al, 2019; Dicken, 2010; Elleuch & Taktak, 2015).

2.2 Theories of Globalization

Globalization, as a complex phenomenon and one of the major 21st century concepts, features new systems of finance, production, and consumption in every country, including an integrated worldwide economy involving new transnational cultural patterns and practices, and a global political process influenced by multinationals, trade liberalization and free movement of people. The consequential levels of inequality, domination, and exploitation among countries in the global system are, however, a divisive factor among globalization theorists. Moreover, findings from scholarly literature show there is no common agreement on the effects of globalization (Brown & Bulman, 2006; Calle et al, 2019; Dicken, 2010; Elleuch & Taktak, 2015; Glyn, 2007; Gola & Spadafora, 2011). Our understanding of globalization therefore depends on the preferred theoretical perspectives as discussed below:

2.2.1 World-system Theory

A key structure of the world-system paradigm is capitalism, which divides the world into three hierarchically-organized tiers vis-a-vis: the **developed system** (consisting of countries in Western Europe, North America, and Japan); the **periphery** (comprising of "developing countries" in Asia (Pilbeam., 2001), South America and Africa and in other continents that are still in their formative years within the capitalist system such as China, Saudi Arabia, Chile, South Africa etc) (Liu & Ren., 2012); and **semi-periphery** (made of countries that were previously among the developed nations but are currently moving down the hierarchy e.g. Germany.

A key feature of this globalization theory is that values flow through the core, semi-periphery, and periphery in a cyclic manner, with each segment playing specific roles in the international division of labour. This exploitative functionality creates room for perpetual domination and inequality among nations (Bond, 2019; Hardt & Antonio, 2007; Husein, 2019).

Additionally, this centralized network functions with structures that promote reproduction of global economic and socio-political systems but breeds inter-state rivalry. Proponents of the world-system theory are of the opinion that the structure favours developed economic and does not recognize "under-developed" or "peripheral" nation-states as an influential part of the larger global system. According to Arrighi (2005), the global system is characterized by increasing industrialization, trends to expand regional/global influence, supremacy battle among core powers, and an unending cataclysmic struggle between anti-systemic forces (Harvey, 2007; Iu, 2005; Kousenidis, 2017).

2.2.2 GLOBAL CAPITALISM THEORY

Proponents of this theory focus on the historical process that laid foundation for the current global economic structures discussed above. The global capitalism theory, according to Sklair (2000), therefore views globalization as the first phase of world capitalism—with emphasis on features that distinguish the old and new eras such as the IMF and World Bank whose activities cannot be influenced by inter-state systems or nation states. Sklair (2002) adds that transnational practices (TNPs) are at the core of this globalization theory, noting that the originators of TNPs are non-state actors which activities span across national boundaries. TNPs are, thus, categorized into three: the **"political"** which is controlled by translational capital or the transnational class (TCC); the **"cultural/ideological"** which is defined by the cultural elites; and the **"economical"** which revolves around **transnational capital.**

Practices in each of the three phases are regulated a major system such as the IMF. In Sklair's opinion, TCCs act as a unifying system for different social groups (CEOs and management of multinational corporations, politicians, globalising bureaucrats, consumerist elites, professionals etc) with individual interests that are embedded in a constantly evolving global capitalist system (Levitt, 2001; Liu & Ren, 2012; Mansor et al, 2019). The rise of TCC as an influential player in the integrated international market explains how globalization divides people and determines class relations within local communities, cities, regions and countries across the globe, also setting up class structures which has been a long-standing cause of class conflicts as well as political, military and economic alliances (Abdul Samad, 2014; Marcuse & & van Kempen, 2000).

2.2.3 Theory of Global Culture

This theory of globalization examines ideologies, belief systems and cultural patterns that are widely accepted as a "global culture." Proponents of the global culture theory view the world as a single place of global village (Marcuse & van Kempen., 2000). Emphasis is, however, on the rising influence of ICT and social media in recent decades. Levitt (2001) identified some of the major concepts under the global culture theory as globalization, globalization of tourism, nations, religion, ethnicity, and global communications. Individuals, in this context, use the entire world as their reference point rather than their local communities or nation-states (Ahmed & Brennan, 2019).

Global consciousness is therefore a key feature of the global culture theory. For example, "hybridization" refers to the fusion of dissimilar cultural patterns to form new, constantly evolving trends in social systems around the world (Arrighi, 2005). But a major problem of the global culture theory is lack of specific representation or identity in the new global system, which Appandurai (1990) called a "disjunctive order" due to inexistent links between politics, culture, and economy.

Conclusion: In line with arguments from proponents of the IMF and globalization, recent trends in world economic development show there are more benefits than losses from civilization and modernization (Harvey., 2007). My future theoretical work will therefore examine systemic changes in social action and inter-governmental power relations in this globalization age, including the challenges posed by authoritarianism, global terrorism, ecological degradation, and militarism.

Chapter 3

3.1 An Overview of the IMF

The IMF is a union of 189 nations with shared interest on fostering improved monetary cooperation, safe and stable financial system, sustainable economic growth, poverty reduction and employment. Founded in 1944 to promote free trade among member countries, IMF's major achievement is the institutionalization of a trusted system of exchange rates and cash payments across national frontiers. In 2012, the Fund's objectives were enhanced to include elements in the financial and macroeconomic sector that have consequences on world stability (Hardt & Antonio., 2007; Amal & Kang, 2019; Ban, 2015).

Figure 1: The IMF at a glance.

1944	Year the IMF was established	**$1 trillion**	Total amount the IMF is able to lend to its member countries
189	Member countries	**36**	Current lending arrangements
150	Nationalities represented by staff	**0%**	Interest rate on loans to low-income countries
24	Executive Directors representing 189 member countries	**$303 million**	For hands-on technical advice, policy-oriented training, and peer learning

Source: The IMF (2019)

3.2 How the IMF Contributes to the Development of Global Trade

The fundamental objective of the IMF is to stabilize global monetary system. It achieves this purpose in three ways vis-a-vis: monitoring global economic trends of member countries; lending fund to countries with trade imbalance; and rendering practical help to struggling members. These processes are discussed below:

3.2A Economic Surveillance

"Surveillance" in this context refers to the IMF's process of watching and dialoguing with individual member countries on the most effective financial and economic policies that are capable of sustaining development. A look at the organization's articles of agreement (Article IV) shows that the IMF has rights to monitor global exchange rate. This cumbersome activity requires a thorough study of member countries' policy strategy and general economic environment. Towards achieving this goal, the IMF sends a group of analysts to each member country once every year and the results are published—with consent from the government. Such published articles are found in "Global Financial Stability Report" and "World Economic Outlook" (Mosco & Mosco., 2019; Appadurai, 1990; Martinez-Diaz & Lamdany, 2009; Mugarura, 2016)

Economic Surveillance: A Case of Vietnam

After decades of war in the 1980s, Vietnam downgraded to one of the world's poorest economies. The southeast Asian country's centrally planned economy could hardly cater for the populace (Pilbeam., 2001). There was dearth of consumer foods, the inflation was as high as 400%, and electric power supply was near zero. Almost everything, including staple foods, were rationed, with poverty and malnutrition ending few lives that had survived the long period of war until 1986, when an IMF-led economic reform "Doi Moi" made a significant impact in the Vietnamese economy through price control, limited subsidies to ailing state-owned firms, increased interest rates, and currency devaluation. Foreign investments gradually flowed in and by 1993, an 8% reduction in inflation rate was documented from nearly 400% in the 1980s. Global trade volumes also skyrocketed, with more citizens traveling abroad—a change which indicated rise of the new middle class (Ashraf, 2013; Birdsall, 2011; Mosco & Mosco, 2019).

IMF reports show that over 40 million people (between early 1990s and 2014) experienced a positive change in their socio-economic status. The country's poverty rate also reduced from 60% to about 14% and life expectancy increased. Remarkably, the nation's per capita growth rate has been the world's fastest—second only to China—with about 5.6% rate recorded every year up to 2017. According to Vo Tri Thanh, a senior expert at the Central Institute for Economic Management, Vietnam, the cooperation with IMF is responsible for the whole transformative process (Iu., 2005). But it is obvious that poverty reduction and economic development cannot be achieved without stability in the macroeconomy (Huu Thu et al, 2020; Mobekk & Spyrou, 2002; Assche & Gangnes 2019).

The IMF should not, however, take credit for Vietnam's path to development because the nation had a determined, accountable, and visionary leadership whose development objectives were supported by hard work of the citizenry. In addition to the public support from a starving population (totalling about 95 million as at 2018), Vietnam also gained financial and technical assistance from the World Bank, Asian Development Bank as well as foreign governments and NGOs. Admittedly, the extra assistance would be nearly impossible without improved credit ratings which attracted FDIs—thanks to IMF advisers who worked tirelessly to improve Vietnam's tax policy, statistics-gathering processes, public administration and central banking system, among others (Howell., 1995; Baldursson & Portes, 2018; Huu Thu et al, 2020).

With the benefits of globalization and cooperation, and support from the IMF, Vietnam implemented privatization policies, particularly in the agriculture sector which has since become its major GDP earner. Cooperative societies lost ownership to lands and individual households were empowered, with market incentives that encouraged large-scale hiring of workers and production of food items as well as regulated pricing which boosted the industry and opened doors for foreign investors. With these achievements, Vietnam was inducted into the Association of Southeast Asian Nations in 1995 and trade agreements (bilateral and multilateral) were signed with regional and global associations leading to the 2007 watershed: its membership of the World Trade Organization (Smith & Guarnizo, 1998; Sklair, L. 2002; Sengul, 2018; Dang et al, 2020; Huu Thu et al, 2020).

Nonetheless, Vietnam has suffered high levels of deforestation and pollution (air and water) due to globalization. On this premise, the country's geographical location few thousands of kilometres away from the coastline makes it vulnerable to climate change (Assche & Gnagnes., 2019; Rivie, 2023; Nguyen-Vo, 2024).

3.2B LENDING

The IMF has an objective to correct underlying developmental problems in ailing member countries by providing loans used to strengthen international reserves, pay for imported goods, lay foundations for economic growth, settle debts, and stabilize currencies (Yeoh, 2015).

IMF LENDING: THE CASE OF IRELAND

Ireland experienced economic recession in 2008, with unemployment rate comparable only to the 1930s Great Depression. By the end of 2010, over 30,000 workers were downsized, and thousands migrated to neighbouring EU countries for job hunt. However, an IMF-led intervention had huge impacts, particularly on the employment rate which slumped to 7% as at 2017—a remarkable change from 15% in 2011. Patrick Honohan, former Central Bank Governor (2009 – 2015) attributed this economic transformation to IMF and European Union's adjustments in the international financial markets (Gola, C. & Spadafora., 2011; Mansor et al., 2019).

IMF's surveillance strategy identified Ireland's problems to be homegrown and "homegrown solutions" were proffered through bank restructuring and debt settlement, including financial and strategic advice which, notably, were coordinated by the Irish government—with minimal interference (Baldursson & Portes., 2018). But prior to 2007, Ireland (once referred to the Celtic Tiger) was one of Europe's fastest growing economies mainly due to low corporate taxes and availability of young, educated workers earning moderate wages from multinational companies such as Coca-Cola, Microsoft, and Dell, which spearheaded manufacturing and export of consumer goods across Europe and the globe. In time, internet, and social media giants such as Google and Facebook, including fund managers and pharmaceutical companies, joined in the competition for Ireland's growing market. Migrant labour increased and the EU country documented a growth rate above 6% per year (Mugarura, 2016; Sklair, 2000; Allen et al, 2013).

Findings, however, show that part of what triggered the crisis were leadership incompetence, available cheap credits, rising wages—thanks to EU's adoption of a common currency "the Euro"—and complacency among financial regulators and banks. By the second half of 2008, investments in real estate suddenly crumbled with low liquidity ratio, scaring foreign investors away. On the other hand, expenditure on social services increased whereas tax revenue fell by 20%, highlighting a deep fiscal, domestic and financial crisis (Mansor et a., 2019; Zoega, 2018; Cohen et al, 2015).

Having accepted IMF's austerity measures, the Irish government on 30 September 2008 announced liability of six major banks. Two years later, capital fund worth €46bn (an estimated 30% of the GDP) was injected into the economy and two out of the six banks were nationalized, notably the Anglo-Irish Bank, which was enmeshed in fund misappropriation scandal. According to Gola, C. and Spadafora (2011), other banks received huge chunks of emergency loans from the European Central Bank (ECB) to stay afloat and support the economic development drive (Elleuch & Taktak., 2015). By the end of 2010, loss of confidence among investors and the government's poor creditworthiness led to capital flight valued above €60bn—a situation which required urgent help from the IMF (Mansor et al., 2019; Samiee, 2019; Cohen et al, 2015).

Cooperation and independent assessment between the IMF, ECB, and European Commission (EC) helped in identifying the value of bad loans and stabilizing the banking system to restore investor confidence—a sine qua non for economic resurgence. The financial/political institutions doled out €24bn to revive the Irish economy although part of the adjustment plan included reduction of wages, implementation of personal income tax, downsizing in the public sector, and institutionalization of bankruptcy law which eased the cumbersome process of loan recovery and encouraged out-of-court settlements. Banks were ordered to upgrade their skills and resources required in the area and, by December 2015, remarkable achievements as the economy bounced back into the global capital markets (Elleuch & Taktak., 2015; Cohen et al, 2015).

One takeaway from the Ireland example is that corporate governance, accountability, and transparency are required to achieve economic growth by ensuring that developmental funds are not misused. But IMF's pro-liberalization conditionality leaves member countries vulnerable to manipulations (Dicken., 2010). Thus, according to the Bank of England, most countries no longer wish to borrow from the IMF, particularly because they have no need to borrow (Pilbeam, 2001; Calle et al., 2018).

3.2C CONDITIONAL LOANS AND/OR STRUCTURAL ADJUSTMENT

During economic recessions, the IMF offer loans to countries that agree on its lending terms and conditions which include tightening of monetary policy by implementing economic programs that are capable of reducing inflation, among other financial measures such as higher tax, removal of price controls, free trade, currency devaluation, and other supply-side policies (e.g. deregulation, privatization, and revitalization of tax collection outlets) (Zoega., 2018; Chletsos & Sintos, 2022; Morgan & Murtagh, 2012; Féliz, 2023).

IMF INTERVENTION: THE CASE OF ICELAND

In the build-up to the 2008 global financial crisis, a prosperous Icelandic economy which relied on free flow of finance to national banks suffered huge current account deficit and external debts. Icelandic banks lost creditors' money to sudden capital flights and eventually defaulted their repayment plans (Yeoh., 2015). The consequence of this credit crunch was unavoidable inflation and increased interest rates which led to loss of confidence in the Icelandic economy (Baldursson. & Portes., 2018).

According to Kousenidis (2017), the IMF promptly responded with financial assistance, doling out a total of $2.2bn as loan package to help revive Iceland's financial sector. The 2-year stand-by loan agreement between both parties was earmarked for an agreed economic program that would stabilize national currency and restore confidence in the Icelandic banking system. This third function of the IMF is called "capacity development" because it aims at strengthening both human and institutional capacity of members, particularly those with scare resources, past/recurring policy failures, and weak institutions. Through capacity development, the global financier revives sectors of the economy, creates jobs, and improves economic growth—where funds are not embezzled or policy processes disregarded (Mugarura., 2016; Cohen et al, 2015).

While working with Iceland, IMF's management also held meetings with other countries affected by the global crises, proposing new lending programs and advising governments on how to adapt to changing and unfavourable economic trends (Ban., 2015). The IMF therefore provides stability in the global monetary system by monitoring economies of member countries to ascertain stability risks, encouraging use of proper technical assistance programs, and providing loans needed to implement new structural adjustment strategies (Zoega., 2018; Hoti & McAleer, 2005). This activity (widely known as economic surveillance) at national or global levels requires synchronization of a country's economic policies with IMF's objectives (Brown & Bulman., 2006; Musleh Alsartawi, 2019; Howell, 1995).

Chapter 4

4.1 Challenges of the IMF

Questionable integrity of the international financial system presents daunting challenge to global peace and stability. This study identified the following as some of IMF's challenges:

4.1.1 Organizational effectiveness

The IMF is poorly rated due to its unreliable capacity for initiating timely, effective solutions to economic problems. In emergency cases, a caucus of G7 network manages such responsibility in private sessions and this procedure makes the IMF a somewhat oppressive tool for the superpowers (Abdul Samad., 2014).

Additionally, the United State wields excessive power in the IMF and this exclusive privilege allows it to manipulate activities of the organization for political purposes (Birdsall., 2011). For example, IMF member-countries contribute funds to run the organization. Though the amounts vary and could increase throughout individual countries' membership—according to size and strength of the economy, the IMF encourages nations to save more. Between 1950 and 2015, the fund skyrocketed from \$50bn to \$300bn. But the US contributes a major share and hold 16% voting rights whereas the UK holds 4% only. This privilege and imbalance highlight the impact of "big spenders" on IMF's decision-making processes (Ban., 2015).

4.1.2   A complex governance structure

The governance structure of IMF is marked by "multiple principals" considered worse than any normal bureaucratic organization. By implication, activities of the IMF are controlled by governments—a circumstance which breeds prolonged arguments, deliberations, and delays in the decision-making process (Sengul., 2018). According to Martinez-Diaz and Lamdany (2009), it is always difficult for countries to agree on what to do, when and how to do it. This implies that organizational performance of the IMF is limited because its aims, objectives and processes are always a result of negotiations among countries with dissimilar interests (Ashraf., 2013; Salehi & Azami, 2019).

However, the global financier has taken some informal governance decisions on countries that defaulted loan agreements in the past. In addition, the IMF has also rendered quick financial help to ailing economies, thus, highlighting flexibility of administrative departments although this approach has been criticised for lack of transparency (Brown & Bulman., 2006).

Figure 2: IMF governance structure

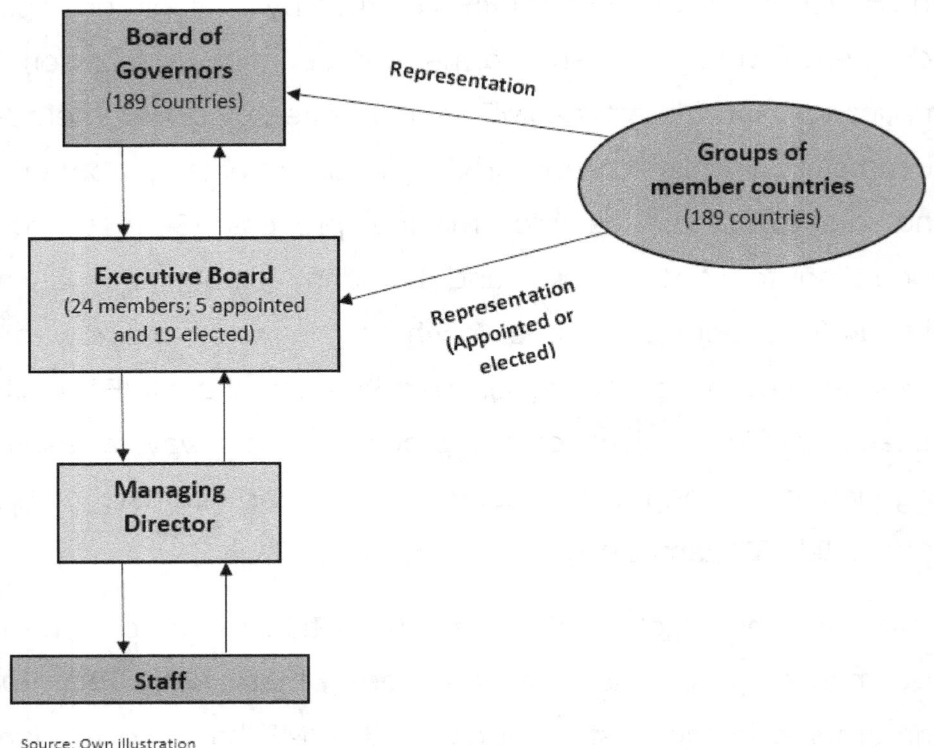

Source: IMF (2019)

4.1.3 Corruption

Corrupt practices are another major challenge to the activities of IMF because there are no strong standards for evaluating performance (Salehi & Azami, 2019). This makes the organization irresponsible for errors committed by its member countries and other stakeholders. Additionally, duplication of roles played by the Board and Management makes IMF's monitoring process cumbersome and ineffective (Mansor et al., 2019; Musleh Alsartawi, 2019). For example, the financial body's gross expenditure has been a source of controversy and discontentment among member-countries. Annual report for the fiscal year 2007 showed the IMF Board spent $59m as administrative costs (a total of $73m when expenditure for the Secretary's Office is included). According to a 2008 report from the Independent Evaluation Office (IEO), this administrative cost which gulped around 6 to 6.5 of IMF's net total between 2008 - 2006 is outrageous and wasteful because the Board can function with lesser amounts. Unfortunately, there are no structures for rewards, punishments, or assessment of how IMF uses organizational resources. This shortcoming is attributed to the overlapping roles played by the Board and management of IMF (Salehi & Azami, 2019; Kousenidis., 2017; Musleh Alsartawi, 2019).

Chapter 5

5.1 Why Developing Countries Hate the IMF

From 9 to 15 October 2023, the International Monetary Fund and the World Bank held their annual joint meeting in Marrakech (Morocco). The last time that these two Bretton Woods institutions met on African soil was in 1973, when the IMF–World Bank meeting was held in Nairobi (Kenya). Kenya's then President Jomo Kenyatta (1897–1978) urged those gathered to find 'an early cure to the monetary sickness of inflation and instability that has afflicted the world'.

Kenyatta, who became Kenya's first president in 1964, noted that, 'over the last fifteen years, many developing countries have been losing, every year, a significant proportion of their annual income through deterioration of their terms of trade'. Developing countries could not overcome the negative terms of trade in a situation where they sold raw materials or barely processed goods on the world market while being reliant on the import of expensive finished commodities and energy, even if they raised their volumes of export. 'Recently,' Kenyatta added, 'inflation in the industrial countries has led to further and important losses to the developing countries.

'The whole world is watching,' Kenyatta said. 'This is not because many people understand the details of what you are discussing, but because the world looks to you to find urgent solutions to problems affecting their daily lives.' Kenyatta's warnings went unheeded. Six decades after the meeting in Nairobi, the loss of national income to debt and inflation remains a serious problem for developing countries. But, in our time, the whole world is not watching.

Most people do not even know that the IMF and World Bank met in Morocco, and few expect them to solve the world's problems. That is because, across the globe, people know that these institutions are, in fact, the authors of pain and are simply not capable of solving the problems that they have created and exacerbated.

Ahead of the meeting in Morocco, Oxfam issued a statement that strongly criticised the IMF and World Bank for 'returning to Africa for the first time in decades with the same old failed message: cut your spending, sack public service workers, and pay your debts despite the huge human costs.' Oxfam highlighted the economic crisis facing the Global South, pointing out that 'more than half (57 percent) of the world's poorest countries, home to 2.4 billion people, are having to cut public spending by a combined $229 billion over the next five years. On top of this, they showed that 'low- and low-middle income countries will be forced to pay nearly half a billion dollars every day in interest and debt repayments between now and 2029'.

Though the IMF has said that it plans to create 'social spending floors' to prevent cuts in government spending on public services, Oxfam's analysis of 27 IMF loan programmes found that 'these floors are a smokescreen for more austerity: for every $1 the IMF encouraged governments to spend on public services, it has told them to cut six times more than that through austerity measures. The fallacy of 'social spending floors' has also been demonstrated by Human Rights Watch in its recent report, Bandage on a Bullet Wound: IMF Social Spending Floors and the COVID-19 Pandemic.

Studies like this paper have continued to monitor the IMF's impact on developing economies, How the International Monetary Fund Is Squeezing Pakistan (October 2023). Written and researched by Taimur Rahman and his colleagues at the Research and Publications Centre (Lahore, Pakistan), the dossier lays out the structural problems facing Pakistan's economy, such as low productivity in its export-oriented industry and the high costs of imported luxury goods. Because of the lack of investment in industry, Pakistan's labour productivity is low, and so its exports are priced out by other countries (as is the case with the textile industry in Bangladesh, China, and Vietnam).

Meanwhile, the import of luxury goods would be far more devastating for the economy if not for the dollars earned by remittances from hard work but ignored Pakistani workers, particularly those in the Gulf states. Pakistan's ballooning deficit, the dossier explains, is 'driven by the fact that Pakistan is no longer competitive in the international market and has continued to import goods and services at a rate that it simply cannot afford.' Furthermore, 'IMF-imposed conditions have further dried up the investment that Pakistan sorely needs to upgrade its infrastructure and accelerate industrialisation.' Not only does the IMF prevent investment for industrialisation, but it enforces cuts on public services (importantly, for health and education).

In July, the IMF approved a $3 billion stand-by agreement with Pakistan that it claimed would create 'the space for social and development spending to help the people of Pakistan'. However, the IMF is simply feeding Pakistan the same tired neoliberal package, calling for 'greater fiscal discipline, a market-determined exchange rate to absorb external pressures, and further progress on reforms related to the energy sector, climate resilience, and the business climate' – all measures that will exacerbate the crisis. To ensure the permanency of these policies, the IMF spoke not only with the government of Caretaker Prime Minister Anwaar-ul-Haq Kakar, but also with former Prime Minister Imran Khan (who was removed from office in 2022 in a move that was encouraged by the United States due to his neutrality on the war in Ukraine). As if these were not enough, through its role facilitating the agreement, the US government pressured the Pakistani government to supply weapons to Ukraine in secret through the disreputable arms dealer Global Ordnance. This makes an already bad deal even worse.

Similar deals have been made with countries such as Argentina, Sri Lanka, and Zambia. In the case of Sri Lanka, for instance, the institution's senior mission chief for the country, Peter Breuer, described the IMF agreement as a 'brutal experiment.' The social consequences of this experiment will, of course, be borne by the

Sri Lankan people, whose frustrations have been stifled by the police and military forces.

This dynamic was also on display in February in Suriname, where large numbers of people who took to the streets to protest the IMF-imposed austerity regime were met with tear gas and rubber bullets. Since the start of the COVID-19 pandemic, Suriname has defaulted three times on its foreign debt, which is owed to wealthy bondholders in the West, and in December 2021 the government of President Chan Santokhi told the IMF that it would cut subsidies for energy. We zijn Moe ('We Are Tired'), a movement against austerity, protested for years but could not move an agenda against the IMF-imposed starvation politics. 'A hungry mob is an angry mob,' Maggie Schmeitz wrote of the protests.

These protests – from Suriname to Sri Lanka – are the latest cycle in a long history of IMF riots, such as those that began in Lima (Peru) in 1976 and sprung up in Jamaica, Bolivia, Indonesia, and Venezuela in the years that followed. When the IMF riots unfolded Indonesia in 1985, long-time CEO of the Bank of America Tom Clausen was presiding over the World Bank (1981–1986). In remarks that he made five years prior, Clausen encapsulated the attitude of the Bretton Woods institutions towards such popular uprisings, stating that 'When people are desperate, you have revolutions. It is in our own evident self-interest to see that they are not forced into that. You must keep the patient alive, because otherwise you cannot effect the cure.'

Clausen's 'cure' – privatisation, commodification, and liberalisation – is no longer credible. Popular protests, such as those in

Suriname, reflect the broad awareness of the failures of the neoliberal agenda. New agendas are needed that will build upon the following ideas, such as:

- ✓ Cancelling odious debts, namely those taken by undemocratic governments and used against the well-being of the people.

- ✓ Restructuring debt and forcing wealthy bondholders to share the burden of debts that cannot be fully repaid (without wreaking devastating and fatal social consequences) but from which they benefited for decades.

- ✓ Investigating the failure of multinational corporations to pay their fair share of taxes to poorer nations and establishing laws that prevent forms of theft such as transfer mispricing.

- ✓ Investigating the role of illicit tax havens in allowing elites in the poorer nations to ferret away the social wealth of their countries in these places and procedures to return that money for public usage.

- ✓ Encouraging the poorer nations to take advantage of new lenders that are not committed to austerity-debt forms of lending, such as the Peoples Bank of China and the New Development Bank.

✓ Developing industrial policies that are geared toward creating jobs, lessening the destruction of nature, and progressively adopting renewable energy sources.

✓ Implementing progressive taxation (especially on profit) and a living wage to ensure fair income for workers as well as wealth distribution.

This list is not comprehensive. If you have other ideas for a credible 'cure,' do write to me.

The photograph featured in this paper is by Ali Abbas ('Nad E Ali'), a visual artist based in Lahore, Pakistan, whose work explores themes of alienation, belonging, and the in-between spaces that exist in all cultures. The photograph is from his series 'Hauntology of Lahore' (2017–present), borrowing the term from philosopher Jacques Derrida. In Abbas's words, 'within the very landscape of

Lahore, amidst its bustling streets, ancient structures, and vibrant communities lies a reservoir of untapped futures and unrealised potential.'

5.2 Does the IMF Truly Care About Less Developed Countries (LDCs)?

Quito's streets tremble between aspiration and repression; the smell of tear gas and the shouts for freedom reverberating in equal measure from one part of the city to another. President Lenín Moreno's State of Emergency (October 3, 2019) and Curfew (October 12, 2019) give the men with guns more authority, but – despite hundreds of injured protestors and at least five dead – the violence has not broken the enthusiasm on the streets. The protests continue. Moreno's options will soon run out. The oligarchy and the International Monetary Fund (IMF) – with a wink from the White House – might ask him to resign. They like their comprador to be credible.

On 13 October, Moreno had to promise to withdraw Decree 833. Pressure from the streets, from the United Nations, and from the Ecuadorian Episcopal Conference forced him to the table, where a televised discussion was held. The Indigenous leaders won the 'debate' – they were much more prepared and far more humane than the president and his clumsy ministers. Moreno and his team – Minister of Government María Paula Romo and Minister of Défense Oswaldo Jarrín – left the room for a recess and surrendered. This is a triumph for the people. But now Moreno must go to the IMF. What pressure will it put on him? The battle continues.

The IMF's board gathers in Washington, DC for its annual meeting. The Fund's new leader is Kristalina Georgieva – from Bulgaria – who used to be at the World Bank. Her job is not easy. The IMF's World Economic Outlook, published in July, calculates that 2019 world output is expected to shrink to 3.2%, compared to 3.8% (2017) and 3.6% (2018). To remain optimistic – with little data to support this attitude – the Fund estimates that world outlook will rise to 3.5% in 2020. But Georgieva and her associates on the Fund's board know that matters are far grimmer. 'Global economic growth continues to disappoint,' Georgieva said recently. Trade wars and high debt levels contribute further to a general crisis of capitalism.

The new Trade and Development Report (2019) from the UN Conference on Trade and Development (UNCTAD), published in late September, says that a recession in 2020 is more than likely. Over the past few years, growth rates have been sustained by 'one-off tax cuts and unsustainable deficits, made all the more precarious by a rapid build-up of private debt positions, particularly in the corporate sector.' Meanwhile, 'unemployment figures hide problems of insecure jobs and discouraged workers. Add to this 'disrupted supply chains, volatile capital flows, and rising oil prices,' and it seems inevitable that 'on these trends a slowdown – and possibly even a recession – looks likely.'

There is nothing that the IMF can do. It is beholden to the United States, from whom Georgieva hopes to raise funds towards the IMF's cache of around $1 trillion. The United States continues to dominate the IMF. In 2015, the IMF released a staff study that argued against 'supply-side economics is, suggesting that the policy that suggests tax cuts and budgets cuts does not lead to utopia. Instead, the authors write, tax cuts and budget cuts produce results whose benefits 'do not trickle down.' The implications of this study did not penetrate the upper floors of the IMF, neither the office of the managing director nor the board. It is business as usual at the IMF. Its own economists are not as important as the whispers from the US Treasury Department and the White House.

Late last year, the European Network on Debt and Development (Eurodad) released an important study on IMF loan conditionalities and the impact this has had on health care. The author – Gino Brunswijck – looked at IMF loans to twenty-six countries between 2016 and 2017. In twenty of these twenty-six countries, 'people have gone on strike or taken to the streets to protest against government cutbacks, the rising cost of living, tax restructuring and wage bill reforms pushed by IMF conditionality.' Since the study came out, the people of Argentina, the Czech Republic, Ecuador, Egypt, Haiti, Jordan, Morocco, Pakistan, Sudan, Tunisia, and other countries have taken to the streets. For them, there is no alternative: either they protest, or they starve.

Several important points emerge from the study by the European Network which bear reflection:

In the past few years, the IMF loans come with an increased number of structural adjustment conditions. The average number of conditions per loan between 2017 and 2018 was 26.8; between 2011 and 2013, the average number of conditions per loan was 19.5.

Inside the dense language of the loan, there are a series of 'hidden' conditionalities; these are often in the annex documents for the loan.

Once the loan agreements have been signed, the IMF returns to add more conditions on the same loan.

Of the twenty-six loans studied, twenty-three of them demanded 'fiscal consolidation,' which means that the governments were forced to restrict spending. The IMF, in other words, foisted austerity on these countries.

Most of the countries that went to the IMF were 'repeat borrowers,' which means that the IMF loans did not fix their problems but only exacerbated them. The IMF did nothing to solve the structural insolvency of these governments, but instead loaned the countries into unsustainable debt. In 2013, an IMF study admitted that due to the IMF agreement with Greece in 2010, 'Market confidence was not restored, the banking system lost 30 per cent of its deposits and the economy encountered a much deeper than expected recession with exceptionally high unemployment'. The Fund's demands only deepened Greece's problems. This lesson has not been absorbed.

Finally, the IMF demanded austerity of developing countries even in times of crisis, knowing full well that this is the time when it is important for governments to spend towards fiscal stimulation of a depressed economy. Advanced capitalist countries, on the other hand, do not observe the IMF demand. Between the autumn of 2008 and the start of 2009, calculates the French economist Cédric Durand, these states committed 50.4% of the world GDP to support the financial sector. Nothing of this generosity has ever been committed to support the poor, who make up the vast majority of the planet's people.

Camouflaged behind IMF phrases such as 'forging a stronger social compact' comes the old-fashioned tonic of austerity for the poor, generosity for the rich. The agreement between the IMF and Ecuador called upon Moreno's government to cut wages and to cut 140,000 public sector employees, while energy prices and fees for government services would be raised. The rich would pay none of the price. The money paid to buy gallons of tear gas and riot police equipment could just as easily have been paid out for health care and education. The 'social compact' that the IMF finds itself building in each country is forged not through the bonds of society but through the barricades of protest and repression.

Each IMF chief comes to the top office with a signature agenda. Christine Lagarde wanted to push gender equity, which meant – for Lagarde and the IMF – increasing the number of women in the workforce. In one of the staff papers, the IMF researchers pointed out that this would only be possible if countries invest in infrastructure (such as public transport), promote equal rights for women (such as equal inheritance laws and property rights), and promote access to affordable childcare. But most IMF loan agreements demand cuts in public infrastructure and in childcare and healthcare. IMF policy, in fact, went against even the limited agenda promoted by Lagarde.

Lagarde, who is now in the running to head the European Central Bank, could have done well to listen to Ofelia Fernández, a 19-year-old Argentinian militant who is running for a seat in the Buenos Aires government. Ofelia does not want to define her politics narrowly. She wanted to make it clear to me last month that feminism must accept all the social issues from a feminist perspective – not allow itself to be restricted to 'women's issues,' which are themselves, she pointed out, everyone's issues. In the poorer parts of Argentina, organisations have emerged to fight against the outcome of the crisis. Hunger is a serious issue, with special emphasis on the hunger of children. Most of the leaders of these popular organisations, Ofelia said, are women. Their fight around the economy of care and against austerity must also be seen as a feminist fight. The fight against hunger, Ofelia said, is also feminism.

Georgieva comes to her post eager to tackle 'climate risks' and to urge a move to a post-carbon energy system. Her policy form will be cuts to energy subsidies and a rise in carbon taxes. A recent IMF study shows that gasoline and household energy bills should rise dramatically to limit global warming. What we have here is austerity packaged as environmentalism. Rather than promote a policy slate of regressive taxes on the poor, the IMF could urge more expenditure on public transportation and on a transition from carbon-based energy to more sustainable forms of energy. But this is not the temper of the IMF. Neoliberal policy and austerity are its contours.

The headline of this newsletter does not come from a radical poet. It comes from the Wall Street Journal. During the Asian financial crisis in 1998, the WSJ ran an editorial that said that the IMF 'has not been fighting financial fires but dousing them with gasoline'. The IMF pours the first tranche of gasoline.

People want to douse these flames. Their hopes explode out of the verse of Dennis Brutus (1924-2009), South Africa's anti-apartheid poet:

There will come a time we believe.

when the shape of the planet

and the divisions of the land

will be less important.

We will be caught in the glow of friendship.

A red star of hope

will illuminate our lives.

A star of hope.

A star of joy.

A star of freedom.

5.3 IMF AND CORPORATE GOVERNANCE

Global GDP last year was $87 trillion, up from just $11 trillion in 1980. While GDP is just one among measures of well-being, the improvement is remarkable. But before we start celebrating, consider these numbers, which point to the dark side of the global economy:

$7 trillion

That figure, equal to 8 percent of global GDP, represents the amount of private wealth estimated to be hidden in offshore financial centres, much of which comes from illicit activities.

$1 trillion

That is the gain in government revenue, by one calculation, which could be achieved by reducing corruption around the world by one-third.

These numbers shine a light on the hidden corners of the global economy, the money that escapes the reach of tax collectors, regulators, and law enforcement. These are the ill-gotten gains of graft, the proceeds of regulatory arbitrage, and the profits from tax domiciles that some consider to be the equivalent of tax evasion. Taken together, they detract from the public good. It is money lost that could be used to improve people's lives.

The rise of digital finance, crypto assets, and cybercrime adds to the challenges. Consider the so-called dark web, a hidden marketplace for everything from stolen identities to arms and narcotics.

Illegal or legitimate, these practices have a big impact on government revenues around the world, and increasingly the international community is being called upon to eliminate the regulatory grey areas.

But it is not just a matter of law enforcement. Governments are being pressed to adjust to rapid changes in the global economy that—if properly handled—can bring considerable benefits. That is certainly the case with fintech and, potentially, crypto assets.

Demands on government resources are building—to boost growth in some advanced economies, build infrastructure in emerging markets, and improve health and education in the developing world. So, the draining away of trillions of dollars represents a threat to our well-being. It contributes to a weakening of trust in government and undermines its ability to address key economic problems like inequality and poverty.

IMF research shows that countries with lower levels of perceived corruption have significantly less waste in public projects. And among low-income countries, the share of the budget dedicated to education and health is one-third lower in more corrupt countries. That reduces the effectiveness of social spending.

So how do we address these problems?

That is where the IMF aims to make a difference. The author has co-authored books and journal papers with national authorities, multilateral bodies, and private sector organizations for more than a decade on ways to combat money laundering and the financing of terrorism. His research books on corporate governance and organizational culture have been at the forefront of the effort to strengthen fiscal transparency and, increasingly, to confront corruption.

It comes down to the core notion of governance—how a country defines and implements its economic policies in all their myriad detail and how it adheres to the rule of law. Last year, the IMF adopted a comprehensive framework for enhanced engagement on governance that encompasses the functions most relevant to the economy, things like tax collection, central banking, and financial sector oversight and market regulation.

Improving governance is not easy; it requires sustained effort over the long term. It is not only the right thing to do, but it also brings tangible benefits to millions of people. Joint action will help ensure success.

Chapter 6

5. Conclusion (Findings)

The findings demonstrate that the IMF is as relevant and important as it was when it was created in 1945. However, there is a need for intrinsic and structural changes within this institution to continue discharging its mandate in a changed global regulatory landscape. The IMF is still crucial in fostering a fundamental stabilization function to fragile global economies in areas of financial and technical assistance and developing requisite legal and supervisory infrastructure within fledging member countries.

Some developing countries like China, Vietnam, and Brazil, have taken advantage of globalization. However, in Sub-Saharan Africa, underdevelopment is attributed to neo-colonialism which has been a major cause of terrorism and communal wars (Liu & Ren., 2012). Unfortunately, reversing the trends of modernization in this 21st century is impossible and will not eliminate widespread poverty, according to Mobekk and Spyrou (2002). The IMF therefore needs a new, strategic approach to globalization—better than the 1999 Poverty Reduction Strategy Paper (PRSP)—to improve living standards and close the disparity between rich and poor nations. To achieve this, there is need to promote institution building, international economic cooperation, equity and equality in wealth distribution, and establishment of long-tern development projects, with individual governments recognizing the importance of change and internal reforms.

5.1   Key Recommendations

The numerous challenges faced by IMF can be controlled by improving policy formulation processes, implementation structures, and monitoring mechanisms. These strategies will empower the organization to effectively manage threats from macro-economic systems as well as double its lending power. In 2016, member-countries like Japan ($60bn), S. Korea ($15bn), the UK ($15bn) and Sweden ($10) contributed to consolidate IMF's improved lending abilities (Gurdgiev, 2011). On this backdrop, the researcher recommends:

- ✓ Restructuring of IMF governance considering the dysfunctionality of the quota system, which also serves as a determinant of each country's financial commitment and voting power.

- ✓ Emergent powers and developing markets such as Brazil, China, India, and Türkiye should be integrated in IMF's decision-making processes. As members of G24, these opinions from these countries should be considered and used in both short and long-term plans (Yeoh., 2015).

- ✓ The IMF should adopt a population-based formula to increase member-countries' voting rights and ensure that developing nations get fair and adequate representations in decision-making (Mobekk and Spyrou., 2002).

✓ The current overlap in responsibilities saddled by the Board and management of IMF should be re-examined and minimized to enhance achievement of aims and objectives (Howell., 1995; Musleh Alsartawi, 2019).

✓ The IMF Director also needs to eliminate or reduce politization of the international organization by maximising use of own, legal power when dealing with errant or influential heads of member-countries. Taking a bold stand against governments that seek to use the IMF as a tool for implementing foreign policies is necessary—if the organization will ever regain its public image.

References

"Governance of the IMF: An Evaluation" (2008), Independent Evaluation Office (IEO), IMF

Abdul Samad, M. (2014), "Islamic micro finance: tool for economic stability and social change", Humanomics, Vol. 30 No. 3, pp. 199-226.

Ahmed F. and Brennan L., (2019), "An institution-based view of firms' early internationalization", International Marketing Review, Vol. 36 No. 6, pp. 911-954.

Allen, F., Gu, X. and Kowalewski, O. (2013), "Corporate governance and intra-group transactions in European bank holding companies during the crisis", Global Banking, Financial Markets and Crises (International Finance Review, Vol. 14), Emerald Group Publishing Limited, Leeds, pp. 365-431.

Amal M. and Kang H., 2019, "Outward Foreign Direct Investment and Multinationality of Emerging Multinationals," International Business Research, Vol. 14, pp. 481-505

Appadurai, A. 1990. 'Disjuncture and difference in the global cultural economy.' In M. Featherstone (ed.), Global Culture: Nationalism, Globalization and Modernity, 295–310. Thousand Oaks, CA: Sage.

Arrighi, G. 2005. 'Globalization in world-systems perspective.' In R. Appelbaum and W.I. Robinson (eds.), Critical Globalization Studies, pp. 33–44. New York: Routledge.

Ashraf, D. (2013), "Performance evaluation of Islamic mutual funds relative to conventional funds", International Journal of Islamic and Middle Eastern Finance and Management, Vol. 6 No. 2, pp. 105-121.

Assche A. and Gangnes B., 2019, "Production Switching and Vulnerability to Protectionism," International Business Research, Vol. 14, pp. 69-87.

Baldursson F. and Portes R., 2018, "Restoring Trust in Iceland: Iceland's IMF Programme," IMF Paper, pp. 111-128.

Ban, C. (2015), "From Designers to Doctrinaires: Staff Research and Fiscal Policy Change at the IMF", Elites on Trial (Research in the Sociology of Organizations, Vol. 43), Emerald Group Publishing Limited, pp. 337-369.

Birdsall N., 2011, "IMF Leadership: OK for Now, but Fixing the Process Shouldn't Wait," Centre for Global Development, Available at: http://blogs.cgdev.org/globaldevelopment/2011/09/imf-leadership-ok-for-now-but-fixing-the-process-shouldn%E2%80%99t-wait.php.

Bond P., 2019, "Neoliberal Liberalism → African Authoritarianism → Disorganized Dissent," Class History and Class Practices in the Periphery of Capitalism (Research in Political Economy, Vol. 34), pp. 89-116.

Brown, R. and Bulman, T. (2006), "The evolving roles of the clubs in the management of international debt", International Journal of Social Economics, Vol. 33 No. 1, pp. 11-32.

Calle G., DiCaprio A., Stassen M. and Manzer A., 2019), "Can Blockchain Futureproof Supply Chains? A Brexit Case Study," International Finance Review, Vol. 20, pp. 101-122.

Chletsos, M. and Sintos, A. (2022), "The effects of IMF programs on income inequality: a semi-parametric treatment effects approach", International Journal of Development Issues, Vol. 21 No. 2, pp. 271-291.

Cohen, S., Guillamón, M.-D., Lapsley, I. and Robbins, G. (2015), "Accounting for austerity: the Troika in the Eurozone", Accounting, Auditing & Accountability Journal, Vol. 28 No. 6, pp. 966-992.

Dang, H.D., Dam, A.H.T., Pham, T.T. and Nguyen, T.M.T. (2020), "Determinants of credit demand of farmers in Lam Dong, Vietnam: A comparison of machine learning and multinomial logit", Agricultural Finance Review, Vol. 80 No. 2, pp. 255-274.

Dicken P., 2010, "Global Shift: Mapping the Changing contour of the World Economy (6th eds)," Guilford Press

Elleuch, S. and Taktak, N. (2015), "Earnings management and evolution of the banking regulation", Journal of Accounting in Emerging Economies, Vol. 5 No. 2, pp. 150-169.

Féliz, M. (2023), "Can Debt Be Sustainable, if Life Isn't? Argentina's Debt Crisis and Social Reproduction * ", Sylla, N.S. (Ed.) Imperialism and the Political Economy of Global South's Debt (Research in Political Economy, Vol. 38), Emerald Publishing Limited, Leeds, pp. 23-53.

Glyn A., 2007, "Capitalism Unleashed," Oxford, England: Oxford University Press.

Gola, C. and Spadafora, F. (2011), "Financial Sector Surveillance and the IMF", Batten, J. and Szilagyi, P. (Ed.) The Impact of the Global Financial Crisis on Emerging Financial Markets (Contemporary Studies in Economic and Financial Analysis, Vol. 93), Emerald Group Publishing Limited, Bingley, pp. 255-310.

Gurdgiev, C. (2011), "Chapter 6 Euro's crisis: From the sovereigns to the banks and back to the sovereigns", Leonard, L. and Botetzagias, I. (Ed.) Sustainable Politics and the Crisis of the Peripheries: Ireland and Greece (Advances in Ecopolitics, Vol. 8), Emerald Group Publishing Limited, Leeds, pp. 109-139.

Hardt M. and Antonio N., 2007, "In What Ways is the "New Imperialism" Really New?" Historical Materialism, Vol. 15 (3), pp. 57–70.

Harvey D., 2007, "Neoliberalism as Creative Destruction," The Annals of the American Academy of Political and Social Science, Vol. 610, pp. 22-44

Held D. and McGrew A., 2007, "Globalization/Anti-Globalization (2nd eds)," Cambridge, England: Polity

Hoti, S. and McAleer, M. (2005), "Assessment of Risk Ratings and Risk Returns for 120 Representative Countries", Hoti, S. and McAleer, M. (Ed.) Modelling the Riskiness in Country Risk Ratings (Contributions to Economic Analysis, Vol. 273), Emerald Group Publishing Limited, Leeds, pp. 111-335.

Howell, K.K. (1995), "The evolution and goals of lending to developing countries by the Bank for International Settlements", Journal of Economic Studies, Vol. 22 No. 6, pp. 69-80.

Husein, J.G. (2019), "Foreign aid, workers' remittances and economic growth in Jordan", International Journal of Social Economics, Vol. 46 No. 4, pp. 532-548.

Huu Thu, N., Bao Duong, P. and Huu Tho, N. (2021), "Filling the voids left by the formal sector: informal borrowings by poor households in northern mountainous Vietnam", Agricultural Finance Review, Vol. 81 No. 1, pp. 94-113.

IMF Quotas (2016) IMF, Available at: http://www.imf.org/external/np/exr/facts/quotas.htm

Iu, J. (2005), "The Prospects of a Regional Monetary Institution for the Asia Pacific", Fetherston, T. and Batten, J. (Ed.) Asia Pacific Financial Markets in Comparative Perspective: Issues and Implications for the 21st Century (Contemporary Studies in Economic and Financial Analysis, Vol. 86), Emerald Group Publishing Limited, Bingley, pp. 469-505.

Kousenidis, D. (2017), "The market impact of the involvement of the EU/ECB/IMF in crisis-affected countries during the European sovereign debt crisis", Review of Accounting and Finance, Vol. 16 No. 2, pp. 162-178.

Levitt, P. 2001. The Transnational Village. Berkeley, CA: University of California Press

Liu, Q. and Ren, X. (2012), "Transfer of funds in China-US BIT negotiations: comparing the Articles of Agreement of the IMF", Journal of International Trade Law and Policy, Vol. 11 No. 1, pp. 6-26.

Mansor, F., Al Rahahleh, N. and Bhatti, M. (2019), "New evidence on fund performance in extreme events", International Journal of Managerial Finance, Vol. 15 No. 4, pp. 511-532.

Marcuse, P., and van Kempen, R. 2000. Globalizing Cities: A New Spatial Order? Oxford: Blackwell.

Martinez-Diaz, L. & Lamdany, R. (2009) "Studies of IMF Governance: A Compendium" International Monetary Fund Working Paper.

Mobekk, E. and Spyrou, S. (2002), "Re-evaluating IMF involvement in low-income countries: the case of Haiti", International Journal of Social Economics, Vol. 29 No. 7, pp. 527-537.

Morgan, I.W. and Murtagh, J.P. (2012), "An analysis of global credit risk spreads during crises", Managerial Finance, Vol. 38 No. 3, pp. 341-358.

Mosco V. and Mosco V. (2019), "City of Technology: Where the Streets Are Paved with Data," The Smart City in a Digital World (Society Now), pp. 59-95.

Mugarura, N. (2016), "The IMF, its mandate and influence in prevention of financial sector abuse", Journal of Financial Crime, Vol. 23 No. 4, pp. 987-1011.

Musleh Alsartawi, A. (2019), "Board independence, frequency of meetings and performance", Journal of Islamic Marketing, Vol. 10 No. 1, pp. 290-303.

Nguyen-Vo, T. (2024), "Geoeconomic and foreign policy implications of Vietnam's economic dependency on China", Fulbright Review of Economics and Policy, Vol. ahead-of-print No. ahead-of-print.

Pilbeam, K. (2001), "The East Asian financial crisis: getting to the heart of the issues", Managerial Finance, Vol. 27 No. 1/2, pp. 111-133.

Rivie, M. (2023), "Limits of Sovereign Debt Restructuring Mechanisms and Possible Alternatives", Sylla, N.S. (Ed.) Imperialism and the Political Economy of Global South's Debt (Research in Political Economy, Vol. 38), Emerald Publishing Limited, Leeds, pp. 137-162.

Salehi, M. and Azami, M. (2019), "Structural damage localization through multi-channel empirical mode decomposition", International Journal of Structural Integrity, Vol. 10 No. 1, pp. 102-117.

Samiee S., 2019, "Reflections on global brands, global consumer culture and globalization," International Marketing Review, Vol. 36 (No. 4), pp. 536-544.

Sengul M., 2018, "Organization Design and Competitive Strategy: An Application to the Case of Divisionalization,"

Organization Design, Advances in Strategic Management, Vol. 40, pp. 207-228.

Sklair, L. 2000. The Transnational Capitalist Class. London: Blackwell.

Sklair, L. 2002. Globalization: Capitalism and Its Alternatives. New York: Oxford.

Smith, M.P. and Guarnizo, L.E. (eds.) 1998. Transnationalism from Below. Rutgers, NJ: Transaction.

Yeoh, P. (2015), "The imposing of constraints on capital flows in emerging economies", International Journal of Law and Management, Vol. 57 No. 5, pp. 400-416.

Zoega, G. (2018), "Restoring Confidence in the Aftermath of Iceland's Financial Crisis", Sigurjonsson, T., Schwarzkopf, D. and Bryant, M. (Ed.) The Return of Trust? Institutions and the Public after the Icelandic Financial Crisis, Emerald Publishing Limited, pp. 3-28.

TRANSCRIPT OF IMF MANAGING DIRECTOR'S PRESS BRIEFING ON THE GLOBAL POLICY AGENDA

Ms. Kozack: Good morning, everyone. My name is Julie Kozack. I am the Director of Communications at the IMF. Thank you for joining us today and welcome to the Managing Director's press briefing on the Global Policy Agenda.

As usual, we will begin today with some opening remarks from our Managing Director, Kristalina Georgieva, and then we will move to your questions. Kristalina, the floor is yours.

Ms. Georgieva: Thank you very much, Julie. You are all familiar with this. We present at the Spring and Annual Meetings our policy priorities, and this is what you would see out today. I would like to start by thanking all of you for the work you do, covering these stories that impact the world. We know now over the last years there have been plenty of turbulence in the world economy for you to cover. We had the pandemic, wars, climate disasters, a cost-of-living crisis, but you also have the opportunity to cover remarkable resilience. As you saw from our World Economic Outlook on Tuesday, despite these multiple shocks and tight financial conditions, growth is firmly in positive territory, and we have slightly upgraded our forecast for this year to 3.2 percent. Yet, there is plenty to worry about. Inflation is down, but not gone.

In the U.S., strong economic performance has a flip side. Disinflation is taking longer than expected. Medium-term growth prospects at around 3 percent are the lowest in decades, held back by a broad-based slowdown in productivity. And divergences within and across groups of countries are growing with poorer countries falling even further behind.

In this context, we have the meetings, and we are presenting our Global Policy Agenda, focusing on three priorities. First, rebuilding fiscal buffers. We have long advocated that while central banks pursue return of inflation to target, they can use some help from the fiscal side. Now fiscal restraint is becoming even more important on its own right because fiscal capacity is exhausted in most countries, and that is dangerously up. Last year global public debt edged up to 93 percent of GDP. This is some 9 percentage points above the pre-pandemic level. Debt service is also more expensive, as interest rates have increased.

In a world where crisis keep coming, countries must urgently build fiscal resilience to be prepared for the next shock. As hard as it is, when still part of the population needs support and half of the world is going to the polls, the time has come to adopt medium-term frameworks for fiscal consolidation.

We recognize one-size-fits-all does not fit all. The pace and speed of consolidation will vary depending on country circumstances, so will also the balance between mobilizing revenue and improving spending efficiency. What is very important is not to forget the burden should not fall on the most vulnerable people.

The second priority, to revive growth prospects. Foundational reforms, strengthening governance, cutting red tape, increasing female labour market participation, improving access to capital. They are all essential for growth, and even more so are productivity-enhancing structural reforms and investment in human capital, the green and the digital transition. With artificial intelligence already upon us, coordination on global rules is as important as having the technology and the skills to tap into it.

New efforts to promote and maintain open flows of goods and capital can build on what has worked to lift living standards in the past while being mindful of the need to ensure that the benefits are widely and fairly shared.

We are directing a significant part of our research towards policies to enhance the growth prospects of our members, in particular, those most severely impacted by exogenous shocks. That brings me to the third priority, renewing our commitment to our membership.

Over the last years, the Fund has been there for our members when they need it, as much as they need it. We provided over $300 billion in financial support to almost 100 countries. As many of you have witnessed at the Annual Meetings in Marrakech, our members gave us a strong vote of confidence by increasing our quota resources and injecting concessional funds into the Poverty Reduction Growth Trust and our Resilience and Sustainability Trust. And this month I am very pleased to tell you we have reached our target of $25 billion SDR—this is around US$30 billion—in precautionary balances, our own protection against financial risks.

This financial strength allows us to play our role at the centre of the Global Financial Safety Net at a time of exceptional uncertainty. And we will remain the transmission line for good policies and for global economic cooperation.

I want to finish with this. In a world of more frequent shocks, we know we will be tested again. And to quote Winston Churchill, "This is no time for ease and comfort. It is time to dare and endure." And there we will, as we have done in the past years, to serve our members in the best possible way tailored to their individual needs. And with this, I thank you and we open your floor to your questions.

Ms. Kozack: Very good. We will go around and take questions. I will ask that you please limit your questions to one so that we can get to as many of you as possible. Let us start right here, woman in the dress in the second row at the end here.

Question: Thanks a lot for the opportunity to ask this question. You characterized the mood as resilience in the near term, but in the medium term, as you note, the projections are the worse they have been in decades, you know, that is due to fears about productivity. Could you maybe say a little bit more about what you think of the drivers of that slowdown in productivity, maybe in the explanation a little bit about why you think, say, the likes of the U.S. have performed a little bit better than the likes of, say, the EU? Thank you.

Ms. Georgieva: Thank you for this question. This is what preoccupies us these days, how can we better understand the slowdown of productivity and growth and what we can do to reverse it, what we can do to help countries reverse it.

So, what has happened is on multiple fronts. After the Global Financial Crisis, we have seen somewhat slower accumulation of capital and then the allocation of both labour and capital, not necessarily the most impactful from a productivity standpoint way.

As we are all aware, the last decades before the surge of inflation, it was a time of very low, sometimes even negative interest rates. And a question arises, was that a factor that allowed firms that otherwise may not have been competitive to stay afloat? We have seen the way technology penetrates the economy, bringing some gains but not the level of gaining that we thought we might see. And over the last years, there is a little bit of self-inflicted injury. Fragmentation means that what otherwise would have been more optimal allocation of capital may not be so. I also would say this. In many countries, aging populations, labour force that does not bring dynamism that can help growth go up. In other words, we have multiple factors affecting productivity and growth. Among them, sometimes countries being shy to take forward reforms that would help productivity but may be difficult to carry.

So, to wrap it up, there are multiple reasons for slowing—for productivity and growth slowing down. And, of course, we know that productivity slowdown is not the whole reason why growth is slowing down. There are also other factors, and I mentioned some of them.

So, you ask a very interesting question. Why is the U.S. doing better than Europe? And when we look at the U.S., there are three things that distinguish the U.S. economy. One is the force of innovation and how easy it is for innovation to turn into business development and then to be scaled up. We know that in Europe, there is still work to be done to unleash the power of innovation. Just comparing the cost of a patent in the U.S. and in the European Union tells a story.

Second, the U.S. is benefiting from abundant labour coming across the border. It creates a domestic political problem and not everybody who crosses the border adds positively to the economy, but that labour supply also gave to the United States another comparative advantage. Wages are not pushing up because there is no strong pressure because of the lack of labour on wages growth.

And the third reason is the U.S. has benefited from more favourable conditions in terms of energy prices, something that has been quite a serious factor for Europe, not a positive factor for Europe. So, when we look at the future, if we add to this more investment in human capital, make the labour force more agile and dynamic, and more forceful allocation with capital where it would bring higher productivity, then we can see the picture lightening up.

I do not know whether you heard me—I am sorry, I am drawing— this is what I think, I wake up in the middle of the night and I think how we can help our members lift productivity. I do not know whether you looked at the graph that shows the trajectory of global growth, medium-term prospects for growth. It looks like a Swiss ski slope. And we sure do not want that for the future. OK. Enough on growth. Not enough on growth, but enough on growth for now.

Ms. Kozack: Welcome right here to the woman in black in the second row.

Question: My question is regarding China's economic growth. You just went back from a trip to China. I would love to know more about your takeaways from your trip and from your firsthand experience and observations, how you think China can hit its growth target this year.

Ms. Georgieva: Thank you for your question. I had an opportunity to visit China and discuss with the Chinese leadership how they think about growth prospects for the country and reflect on what we have learned about China. And here are my main takeaways. First, China is on a fork on the road—at the fork on the road. Why? Because China must define growth strategies for the future yet. China has the benefit of a particular set of policies over the last decades, export-oriented growth, but the time has come to look at domestic sources for growth, opening more opportunities for the market to lift these prospects. And at the Fund, we see three important opportunities for China. Number one, to shift the economy more towards domestic consumption. It is in line with what China is aspiring, the dual circulation economy. It would take giving consumers more confidence and offering them more services, more things to buy. We know that the healthcare services in China can expand quite significantly. We know that getting the social safety nets to work more effectively would give people an opportunity to save a bit less, to spend a bit more.

Secondly, we see the reforms in China that have served the country well continuing to be needed, reforms of state-owned enterprises opening for a more competitive environment. In the years ahead, that can help China grow more.

Last but not least, there are some problems right now, and how they are solved will have implications for China's growth. The most obvious example is the property sector. People in China rely on their homeownership as a way of saving. When prices there—as savings go down, when prices of real estate go down, that affects consumer confidence. So, clearing up the problems in the sector more resolutely would certainly help China. And we see China taking some important decisions around greening their growth pattern. Again, the more China does for lifting domestic consumption, the better.

Ms. Kozack: Let us go here in the middle, yes. Gentleman right here in the middle. Yes, the second row.

Question: Thank you. So, the Russian war in Ukraine is continuing to be part of the Global Policy Agenda, and Ukraine is continuing to be targeted by Russian missile attack which targets energy and other infrastructure in Ukraine. So, Ukraine's financial needs are growing now probably more than expected earlier. How does the IMF view Ukraine's current economic budget risks and is the Fund ready to take more steps to strengthen international support for

Ukraine when the situation gradually becomes complicated? Thank you.

Ms. Georgieva: The war above all is a tragedy for people. Having men and women and children killed and wounded is a daily occurrence, so we need this war to end for their sake. And we also need the hands for the sake of the world economy, not just for Ukraine. It adds to geo-economic tensions, and the further they go, the less good are our prospects. Going back to the growth issue, that worsens our prospects to reverse the direction of growth.

Within Ukraine, what we see after years of very close engagement is a remarkable determination of the economic team and of the Ukrainian people to have a functioning economy despite the war. We have a $15.1 billion program with Ukraine. We have completed in March our third review very successfully. And what it shows is that Ukraine has been able to counter the highly disturbing force of the war. Growth is 5.3 percent; inflation, 3.2 percent; and tax collection, around 36 percent of GDP. And I am asking you, how many countries do you know today that have that kind of performance?

We have disbursed a third time under our program, but the most important role of our program—and it goes straight into the answer to your question—is that it is a catalyst for financial support for Ukraine. The program mobilizes $122 billion over 4 years. It gives predictability to the Ukrainian authorities that funding would be there. And I was very pleased to listen to statements yesterday at the roundtable on Ukraine. The support for Ukraine remains steady. It is firm.

You are all aware of the EU 50 billion euros. The U.S. administration is pursuing in Congress support from Ukraine. Many other countries, Japan, Canada, U.K. are stepping up, South Korea. The list is long. You also asked would the needs of Ukraine grow because of the horrific bombing of critical infrastructure? At this point, we assessed the needs for this year at 42 billion. We have confidence that these needs would be met. Of course, we will have to continue to carefully monitor conditions in the country but let me say this. It is the best way to deal with the problem is for the problem, the war to go away. This war, the war in Gaza, the less of this we have as humans, the better. And looking at the women in the audience, the more women we have in the position of authority, the better chance we have for peace.

Ms. Kozack: I will take the gentleman at the very end of the first row, please.

Question: Thank you. Zambia's successfully restructured its debt. So, what does—what interventions does the IMF wish to see to enable that the country does not get back into debit distress, bearing in mind the mounting pressures to raise about $1 billion for humanitarian aid on the people which are affected by the droughts?

Ms. Georgieva: Let me congratulate Zambia for successfully completing very complicated negotiations on debt restructuring with both the official and the private-sector creditors. Bravo. And very timely because, as you indicated in your question, Zambia is experiencing a very dramatic drought. It is affecting food security. It is affecting electricity production. And we all know how shortages of electricity supply, of energy supply overall affect the economy.

I have had many opportunities to meet with the Minister of Finance, with the President of Zambia. I visited the country. It is a country with enormous potential. It has very fertile soil. It has rich natural resources. It is one of the not many countries in Africa with a relatively small population—17 million people on a large territory. And it has a determined leadership to pursue reforms.

A bit about Zambia. I think we will see increase in investments. We also will continue to work with Zambia on economic reforms. We have done something very important. We did a governance assessment as a foundation for anticorruption measures because, as we all know, one of the problems in resource-rich countries is the cancer of corruption. So, removing this cancer is a very important factor to attract financing. And from what we can see, investors are coming to Zambia.

Also, the country has taken a very important decision to invest in its people, making education free and accessible. I went to a school, 80 kids in a small room, four per desk, four per book, textbook. But so eager to learn. So motivated to contribute to their country.

If I ever need a lift of the depressing news you guys deliver, I am going to go to Zambia.

Ms. Kozack: Let us go here, third row, woman in the yellow jacket.

Question: Hello. Considering the wreaks of a division of the world in blocks, how will that affect Latin America and what precaution has the IMF taken? Thank you.

Ms. Georgieva: Thank you for your question. Let us start with where Latin America is. The region has faced problems in reaching dynamic growth, and in fact Latin America is—growth in Latin America is below the average global growth. Indeed, geo-economic fragmentation is a negative factor for everybody, including for Latin America, with some caveats. When you look at Latin America, Mexico benefits from fragmentation because it has become an entry point into the United States for goods that otherwise might have come from point A to point B without going through Mexico. So, there is this element of lengthening supply chains that we are seeing more broadly, and we see some of it in Latin America.

So, what are the opportunities for Latin America? First, to improve what has not worked so greatly in the past. And it is in macroeconomic policies, in some countries being too generous; in other countries being too generous in spending; in other countries being too restrictive. So, get that fiscal monetary financial-sector policies in the best possible shape you can. And we see that countries are looking—I mean, look at Argentina, a country that has been for a long time perceived as a lugger from a reform standpoint of view now is moving very rapidly in tightening the fiscal spending, getting the ability of private investment to find a better return. Inflation in Argentina is going down a little faster than we initially expected.

I want to actually sing a praise also to Latin America in the following. After the Global Financial Crisis, countries have taken to heart getting their monetary policy in order. And many countries in Latin America were faster in tackling inflation than the rest of the world. Now they can start cutting rates. So, it is a complex region. There are different stories. But by and large, I think Latin America can go with more effort on the policy front. Latin America can go up and do much better.

Ms. Kozack: Let us go back to the centre. I will take the woman in the front row in the pink, please.

Question: Thank you, Ms. Georgieva, for taking my question. So, in the MENA region, the economic cycle is quite different than it is globally and with rising inflation again, it is burdening everyone across the globe, especially with the rise in oil prices and commodity prices. Now, my question is, how can the different countries in our region, both oil and non-oil-producing countries, deal with the current contractionary monetary policy with the current strong dollar that is burdening the highly-indebted countries; and how can the IMF support the countries affected by the current Gaza war and the war in South Lebanon as well? Thank you.

Ms. Georgieva: Thank you for bringing in focus the Middle East that has indeed been on the receiving end of more turbulence since October. What we recognize is that this impact of the war is indeed affecting the Middle East. At a time when we have upgraded slightly global projections from 3.1 to 3.2 percent, we have downgraded our projections for growth in the Middle East by 0.7 percent. And that is primarily the result of that uncertainty.

What we see is the most severe impact is felt where the epicentre of the war, West Gaza in particular, also the West Bank, Gaza's economy is wiped out. More than 80 percent is gone. But also, the West Bank is severely impacted. There is some impact on the neighbourhood in the following way: most severe on Lebanon, somewhat less on other countries. I would say Jordan has shown remarkable resilience and so has Egypt. In both cases, in the case—you asked what the IMF can do. In both cases, in Jordan and in Egypt, we have programs. In Jordan, $1.2 billion program that is anchored in Jordan's own reform plans. It does provide a strong buffer for Jordan and, as a result, the impact of the war is generally minimal.

In Egypt, we had a program, $3 billion program. We have done something that is rare. We have augmented the program by 5 billion. It is now an 8-billion program primarily because of the severity of the regional shock.

When we look beyond those, I just want to bring attention to two countries that should get more attention than they currently do, Sudan and Yemen. Sudan is in the—the situation is terrible, so is in Yemen. And what I want to stress is that when we have these highly visible wars, like the one in Ukraine, like the one in Gaza—Israel-Gaza, they overshadow the pain and suffering that is happening in other places. But rest assured, for us at the Fund, all members are benefiting from our support and our attention, as difficult conditions may be.

If I can go back to Latin America, I was searching for the growth number for Latin America in my brain. My brain said ask Julie for this this little sheet of paper.

So, in Latin America, Caribbean, growth last year, 2.3 percent. It slipped to 2 percent. This year it is going to improve marginally to 2.5 percent in 2025. As you can see, way below the global average. So, countries are doing OK, but not great.

Ms. Kozack: I am afraid we have time for just one more question, so I am going to go back to the centre, woman here in the centre, in the plaid jacket, kind of right by the camera. And this will be our last question.

Question: Thank you. Thank you for taking my question. You mentioned the need to address the climate crisis; and while the Resilience and Sustainability Trust is a step forward, to qualify for RST financing, eligible countries must be in concurrent, on-track financing or non-financing IMF-supported program. However, such a requirement restricts a member's access to the RST. Most of the climate-vulnerable countries are not in an IMF program. Is there consideration to either remove that as a requirement, to eliminate it, and why must it be tied to a program? Thank you.

Ms. Georgieva: Let me answer it this way. We are going to review the performance of the RST and then should there be agreement on adjustments. Adjustments will be made. We are not so sure that removing a requirement for a current program at this moment would be justified. And let me explain why. Two reasons. One, because for us to help countries integrate climate in their macro policies, it is helpful to have an active and intense engagement on macro policies overall. So, when we plug recommendations on climate policies, be it mitigation or adaptation or transition, we do it in the context of intense engagement with the country. And that makes our job likely to be more impactful.

Two, right now we have many programs, both financing and non-financial programs. And more countries are coming to us. Sometimes they do not need money, but they do want to use the Fund as an anchor for their macro policies. Most recently, for example, a country in—not in Africa, in the Middle East, Iraq, said we would like to have a non-financial arrangement with the Fund because we would like to benefit from that anchoring that you offer.

We have approved 18 programs so far. We have about 30 countries that have expressed interest. These are countries with financial and non-financial programs, and our ability to respond and our financial capacity is already being stretched.

So, to help the countries the best in my hearts of heart, I think it is more likely to be effective when we have this more intensive— more tight engagement as we currently have. This being said, as we move forward and we build knowledge and expertise in this area, it might become less important to have that close engagement as one of the prerequisites for a successful RST program.

By the way, you are from Africa. Which country? You are from the Caribbean. OK, I love the Caribbean. You guys are—you know that the Caribbean holds one of the most successful IMF programs ever? Barbados, yes, Jamaica, they are both countries that have non-financial arrangement. They both say they are very happy to have these non-financial arrangements because what it does for them is it gives them more attention from the Fund and more access to expertise. So that works. But the short and the long is, we have something that works. We got very quickly to a very strong portfolio of programs. Let us keep it going. Of course, we will revisit, we will assess. And if there is a need for change or conditions for change, I guarantee you, a change will be made.

Ms. Kozack: I am afraid we are going to have—

Ms. Georgieva: Let me say, Africa. You are asking about Africa. So here is—people are saying no because it would be unfair. Sorry.

Ms. Kozack: I think we will need to wrap up now. We will have another opportunity to—

Ms. Georgieva: Tomorrow. Come tomorrow.

Ms. Kozack: —tomorrow to discuss with the MD. We will have another opportunity tomorrow.

Ms. Georgieva: Come tomorrow. Come tomorrow. Come tomorrow. Because then people will say some words about this and about that and it would not be fair. Come tomorrow. We have another press conference, second bite of the apple. The apple will be right here. Please come.

Ms. Kozack: With this, I am going to conclude the press briefing. Thank you, Managing Director for joining us.

Ms. Georgieva: Thank you, everybody.

Ms. Kozack: The transcript will be available later today on IMF.org, and I invite you to join us for the IMFC press conference tomorrow.

Ms. Georgieva: Thank you.

IMF Communications Department

MEDIA RELATIONS

PRESS OFFICER: Keiko Utsunomiya

Phone: +1 202 623-7100**Email:** MEDIA@IMF.org